feeling

talk

judgement

Nikki Giovanni

38522

MORROW QUILL PAPERBACKS
New York   1979

Printed in the United States of America

Library of Congress Catalog Card Number 70-119846

ISBN: 0-688-25294-X

10

Contents

Black Feeling, Black Talk

Black Judgement

1

Black Feeling,
Black Talk

Introduction to Black Feeling, Black Talk

Nikki Giovanni's one hundred pounds or less have the unique capability of blowing you away, even when she is being gentle; thus is the nature of her unquestionable dynamism.

She springs from the Black city of Lincoln Heights, Ohio, where she lived with Gus, Yolande, Gary and Peppe. This family unit resembles the tribes of old in their commitment to unity.

At sixteen she entered Fisk University and, consistent with her inconsistency, graduated at twenty-four. In that period of time she moved from being an Ayn Rand-reading-Goldwater-supporter, through John Killens' Fisk Writers Workshop, to putting SNCC on campus (*after* Stokely said "Black Power"), editing *Élan* (a campus literary magazine) and, after returning to Cincinnati, initiating an awareness of arts and culture in the Black Community. Beginning with the first Cincinnati Black Arts Festival in June 1967 which Nikki planned and saw through to the establishment of The New Theatre, a Black indigenous theatre, she has been a prime mover in the struggle for awakening. She has lectured at The Black History Workshop in Cincinnati, been Youth Day speaker at Reverend Cleage's Church of The Black Madonna in Detroit, and has begun a Black History group in Wilmington, Delaware, where she now lives.

Nikki is undoubtedly an intellectual. But before that she is a Black woman whose uniqueness is merged with the universal Black experience in such a way that all you can say after reading her is "Yeah."

Here she is presented in her first published collection. *Black Feeling, Black Talk* will turn you on. Dig it.

BARBARA CROSBY/1968

Detroit Conference of Unity and Art
(For HRB)

We went there to confer
On the possibility of
Blackness
And the inevitability of
Revolution

We talked about
Black leaders
And
Black Love

We talked about
Women
And Black men

No doubt many important
Resolutions
Were passed
As we climbed Malcolm's ladder

But the most
Valid of them
All was that
Rap chose me

On Hearing "The Girl with the Flaxen Hair"

He has a girl who has flaxen hair
My woman has hair of gray
I have a woman who wakes up at dawn
His girl can sleep through the day

His girl has hands soothed with perfumes sweet
She has lips soft and pink
My woman's lips burn in midday sun
My woman's hands—black like ink

He can make music to please his girl
Night comes I'm tired and beat
He can make notes, make her heart beat fast
Night comes I want off my feet

Maybe if I don't pick cotton so fast
Maybe I'd sing pretty too
Sing to my woman with hair of gray
Croon softly, Baby it's you

4

You Came, Too

I came to the crowd seeking friends
I came to the crowd seeking love
I came to the crowd for understanding

I found you

I came to the crowd to weep
I came to the crowd to laugh

You dried my tears
You shared my happiness

I went from the crowd seeking you
I went from the crowd seeking me
I went from the crowd forever

You came, too

Poem
(For TW)

For three hours (too short for me)
I sat in your home and enjoyed
Your own special brand of Southern
Hospitality

And we talked

I had come to learn more about you
To hear a human voice without the Top Ten in
   the background

You offered me cheese and Horowitz and
It was relaxing
You gave me a small coke
And some large talk about being Black
   And an individual

You had tried to fight the fight I'm fighting
And you understood my feelings while you
Picked my brains and kicked my soul

It was a pleasant evening
When He rises and Black is king
I won't forget you

Poem
(For BMC No. 1)

I stood still and was a mushroom on the forest green
With all the *moiles* conferring as to my edibility
It stormed and there was no leaf to cover me
I was water-logged (having absorbed all that I could)
I dreamed I was drowning
That no sun from Venice would dry my tears
But a silly green cricket with a pink umbrella said
Hello   Tell me about it
And we talked our way through the storm

Perhaps we could have found an inn
Or at least a rainbow somewhere over
But they always said
Only one   Only one more
And Christmas being so near
We over identified

Though I worship nothing (save myself)
You were my savior—so be it
And it was
Perhaps not never more or ever after
But after all—once you were mine

Our Detroit Conference
(For Don L. Lee)

We met in
The Digest
Though I had
Never Known You

Tall and Black
But mostly in
The Viet Cong
Image

You didn't smile

Until we had traded
Green stamps
for Brownie Points

Poem
(For Dudley Randall)

So I met this man
Who was a publisher
When he was young

Who is a poet now

Gentle and loving and
Very patient
With a Revolutionary
Black woman

Who drags him
to meetings

But never quite
Gets around to
saying

I love you

Poem
(For BMC No. 2)

There were fields where once we walked
Among the clover and crab grass and those
Funny little things that look like cotton candy

There were liquids expanding and contracting
In which we swam with amoebas and other Afro-
    Americans

The sun was no further than my hand from your hair

Those were barefoot boy with cheeks of tan days
And I was John Henry hammering to get in

I was the camel with a cold nose

Now, having the tent, I have no use for it
I have pushed you out

Go 'way
Can't you see I'm lonely

Personae
Poem
(For Sylvia Henderson)

I am always lonely
for things I've never had
and people I've never been

But I'm not really
sad
because you once said
Come
and I did
even though I don't like
you

Poem
(For PCH)

And this silly wire
(which some consider essential)
Connected us
And we came together

So I put my arms around you to keep you
From falling from a tree
(there is evidence that you have climbed
too far up and are not at all functional
with this atmosphere or terrain)
And if I had a spare
I'd lend you my oxygen tent

But you know how selfish people are
When they have something at stake

So we sit between a line of
Daggers
And if all goes well

They will write Someday
That you and I did it

And we never even thought for sure
(if thought was one of the processes we employed)
That it could be done

Poem
(No Name No. 1)

And every now and then I think
About the river

Where once we sat
Upon the bank
Which
You robbed

And I let you
Wasn't it fun

Poem
(For BMC No. 3)

But I had called the office
And the voice across the line
Swore up and down (and maybe
all the way 'round)
That you wouldn't be in

Until 11:00 A.M.

So I took a chance
And dialed your phone

And was really quite content
After you said
Hello

But since I had previously
Been taught
By you especially
That you won't say
Hello
More than once

I picked a fight

Black
Separatism

It starts with a hand
Reaching out in the night
And pretended sleep

We may talk about our day
At the office
Then again
Baseball scores are just
As valid
As the comic page
At break fast

The only thing that really
Matters
It that it comes

And we talk about the kids
Signing our letters

YOURS FOR FREEDOM

A Historical Footnote to Consider Only When All Else Fails
(For Barbara Crosby)

While it is true
(though only in a factual sense)
That in the wake of a
Her-i-can comes a
Shower
Surely I am not
The gravitating force
that keeps this house
full of panthers

Why, LBJ has made it
quite clear to me
He doesn't give a
Good goddamn what I think
(else why would he continue to *masterbate* in public?)

Rhythm and Blues is not
The downfall of a great civilization
And I expect you to
Realize
That the Temptations

have no connection with
The CIA

We must move on to
the true issues of
Our time
like the mini-skirt
Rebellion
And perhaps take a
closer look at
Flour Power

It is for Us
to lead our people
out of the
Wein-Bars
    into the streets
into the streets
(for safety reasons only)
Lord knows we don't
Want to lose the
support
of our Jewish friends

So let us work
for our day of Presence
When Stokely is in
The Black House
And all will be right with
Our World

Poem
(No Name No. 2)

Bitter Black Bitterness
Black Bitter Bitterness
Bitterness Black Brothers
Bitter Black Get
Blacker Get Bitter
Get Black Bitterness
              NOW

The True Import of Present Dialogue, Black vs. Negro
(For Peppe, Who Will Ultimately Judge Our Efforts)

Nigger
Can you kill
Can you kill
Can a nigger kill
Can a nigger kill a honkie
Can a nigger kill the Man
Can you kill nigger
Huh? nigger can you
kill
Do you know how to draw blood
Can you poison
Can you stab-a-Jew
Can you kill huh? nigger
Can you kill
Can you run a protestant down with your
'68 El Dorado
 (that's all they're good for anyway)
Can you kill
Can you piss on a blond head

Can you cut it off
Can you kill
A nigger can die
We ain't got to prove we can die
We got to prove we can kill
They sent us to kill
Japan and Africa
We policed europe
Can you kill
Can you kill a white man
Can you kill the nigger
in you
Can you make your nigger mind
die
Can you kill your nigger mind
And free your black hands to
strangle
Can you kill
Can a nigger kill
Can you shoot straight and
Fire for good measure
Can you splatter their brains in the street
Can you kill them
Can you lure them to bed to kill them
We kill in Viet Nam
for them
We kill for UN & NATO & SEATO & US
And everywhere for all alphabet but
BLACK
Can we learn to kill WHITE for BLACK
Learn to kill niggers
Learn to be Black men

A Short Essay
of Affirmation
Explaining Why
(With Apologies
to the Federal Bureau
of Investigation)

Honkies always talking 'bout
Black Folks
Walking down the streets
Talking to themselves
(They say we're high—
or crazy)

But recent events have shown
We know who we're talking
to

That little microphone
In our teeth
Between our thighs
Or anyplace
That may have needed
Medical attention
Recently

My mail has been stopped
And every morning
When I awake
I speak to
Lessy-in-the-wall
Who bangs behind
My whole Rap

This is a crazy country

They use terms like
Psychosis and paranoid
With us

But we can't be Black
And not be crazy
How the hell would anyone
    feel
With a mechanical dick
in his ass
lightening the way
for   whitey

And we're suppose to jack off
behind it

Well I'm pissed
off

They ain't getting
Inside
My bang
or
My brain

I'm into my Black Thing
And it's filling all
My empty spots

Sorry 'bout that,
Miss Hoover

Poem
(No Name No. 3)

The Black Revolution is passing you bye
negroes
Anne Frank didn't put cheese and bread away for you
Because she knew it would be different this time
The naziboots don't march this year
Won't march next year
Won't come to pick you up in a
honka honka VW bus
So don't wait for that
negroes
They already got Malcolm
They already got LeRoi
They already strapped a harness on Rap
They already pulled Stokely's teeth
They already here if you can hear properly
negroes
Didn't you hear them when 40 thousand Indians died
from exposure to
honkies
Didn't you hear them when Viet children died from
exposure to napalm
Can't you hear them when Arab women die from
exposure to isrealijews
You hear them while you die from exposure to wine

and poverty programs
If you hear properly
negroes
Tomorrow was too late to properly arm yourself
See can you do an improper job now
See can you do now something, anything, but move now
negro
If the Black Revolution passes you bye it's for damned
sure
the whi-te reaction to it won't

Wilmington Delaware

Wilmington is a funni negro
He's a cute little gingerbread man who stuffs his pipe
with
Smog and gas fumes and maybe (if you promise
not to tale)
Just a little bit of . . . pot
Because he has to meet his maker each and everyday
LORD KNOWS HE'S A GOOD BOY
AND TRIES HARD
While most of us have to go to church only once a week

They tell me he's up for the coloredman-of-the-year
award
And he'll probably win
(If he'd just stop wetting on himself each and
everytime he
meets a Due-pontee)
LORD KNOWS HE TRIES

Why just the other day I heard him say NO
But he was only talking to the janitor and I believe
they
expect him to exercise some control over the
excretionary
facilities around here
 (But it's a start)

My only real criticism is that he eats his daily
nourishment at the "Y"
And I was taught that's not proper to do in public

But he's sharp, my but that boy is sharp
Why it took the overlords two generations to recognize
that negroes
had moved to the East side of town (which is similar to
but not the same as the wrong side of the tracks)
And here he is making plans for future whites who
haven't even
reclaimed the best land yet

"Don't say nothing Black or colored or look unhappy"
I heard him tell his chief joints
And every bone bopped in place but quick
(He can really order some colored people around—
a sight to behold)
And does a basically good militant shuffle
when dancing is in order

I'd really like to see him party more but he swears
Asphalt is bad for his eye-talian shoes
And we all appreciate eye-tal
don't we

I tried to talk to him once but he just told me
"Don't be emotional"
And all the while he was shaking and crying
and raining blows on
poor black me

So I guess I'm wrong again
Just maybe I don't know the coloure of my
truefriends
As Wilmington pointed out to me himself

But I'm still not going to anymore banquits

The last one they replaced jello with
jellied gas (a Due-pontee speciality; housewise)
And I couldn't figure out what they were trying
to tell me
Wilmington said they were giving me guest treat-meants

But somehow I don't feel welcome
So I'm going to pack my don-key (asswise) and split
before they start to do me favors too

Letter to a Bourgeois Friend Whom Once I Loved (And Maybe Still Do If Love Is Valid)

The whole point of writing you is pointless
and somewhere in the back of my mind I really do
accept that. But on the other hand the whole point
of points is pointless when its boiled all the way down
to the least common denominator. But I was never one
to deal with fractions when there are so many wholes
that cannot be dissected—at least these poor hands
lack both skill and tool and perhaps this poor heart
lacks even the inclination to try because emotion is
and of itself a wasteful thing because it lacks the power
to fulfill itself. And power is to be sought.
I see, after talking with you I did see, that Johnson
sent his storm troopers into Detroit and that's wrong
and the wrong is not what we have done but what
Johnson and all the johnsons before him have done
and it's wrong that we hate but it's even more wrong
to love when neither love nor hate have anything to do
with what must be done. And Rap does love and
maybe he won't tomorrow or the next day and if
he does maybe it won't be with me but if we must love
then I must love you and him and all other people.

Or I must not deal with love at all. And if we are not
to deal with love then we must not deal with emotion
because if not love then we deal with hate or fear
or anxiety or just anything but The Problem which is
what we must deal with if we are to get back to love
and hate and anxiety and all those foolish emotions.
Which is what we're talking about. And you are angry
with me maybe because you think I'll get hurt
(if indeed you care) or maybe because you think
you'll get hurt but not at all because I hate
because you know I don't hate and not because
I'm violent because you know I'm not violent
so perhaps you are not angry at all but just give
slightly a shade left of a good goddamn what the hell
happens to me and whether or not I want to share it
with you and the truth being that I should give
a bout face and act like an adult except that adulthood
has no room for me because adulthood implies another
adult to relate to and there are no adults
only children whose balloons are bursting spit
all over their faces and having never tasted spit
let alone eaten any shit or licked any ass
you think that liquid on your face is rain from Heaven
and maybe you hope if it rains hard enough
all the wrinkles will disappear and the fountain
of youth, having been presented to you by our friend
and neighbor, will be yours for-ever surrounded by
flashing lights on the outside instead of the terrible
hammer inside which beats the sweat or fans the cold
and sometimes buckles your knees. So we move to
needs which must be met and I confess with a smile
on my lips that my needs are far more important to me
than your needs are to me and even though your needs
mean something to me they are only important
insofar as your needs have a need to meet mine.

And your needs lack significance to me when your
need is to get away from me and my needs.
Which is why I'm currently going through a thing
which is the only accurate description of my emotional
goulash, as if you've never been lonely and basically
afraid but recognizing that fear is an invalid emotion
and so is loneliness but being afraid and lonely
nonetheless. I called you but you have a job.
Which is no longer inclusive of me or maybe I just
developed a bad case of paranoia which in the next
thousand years may be understood by all the people
everywhere who can understand how it feels to be
lonely and afraid when there is no place for emotion.
And that has to upset your world which I fully intend
to do even if I don't like doing it because likes or
dislikes have nothing to do with what has to be done
—even to you with whom I'd dearly like to do nothing
at all. My, but you hurt.

I'm Not
Lonely

i'm not lonely
sleeping all alone

you think i'm scared
but i'm a big girl
i don't cry
or anything

i have a great
big bed
to roll around
in and lots of space
and i don't dream
bad dreams
like i used
to have that you
were leaving me
anymore

now that you're gone
i don't dream
and no matter
what you think
i'm not lonely
sleeping
all alone

Love Poem
(For Real)

it's so hard to love
people
who will die soon

the sixties have been one
long funeral day
the flag flew at half-mast
so frequently
seeing it up
i wondered what was wrong

it will go back
to half
on inauguration day
(though during the johnson love
in the pole
was cut
the mourning wasn't
official)

the Jews are seeking
sympathy
cause there isn't one Jew
(and few circumcised women)
in the cabinet
old mother no dick plans
to keep it
bare
it's impossible to love
a Jew

united quakers and crackers
for death, inc.
are back in the driver's seat
it hertz
and i pledge allegiance
to the removal of all
pain

it's masochistic
 (derived from colored
meaning sick to kiss massa)
to love honkies

riderless horses
backward boots
the eternal flame of the flammable
Black Man
who does not plan to screw
honkies to death

it's so easy to love
Black Men
they must not die anymore

and we must not die
with america
their day of mourning
is our first international
holiday

it's a question of power
which we must wield
if it is not
to be wielded
against
us

For
an Intellectual
Audience

i'm a happy *moile*
the opposite of which
is an unhappy
womblie

and the only way you'll ever
understand
this poem
is if you sit
on your ear
three times a day
facing south
justa whistling
dixie
while nikki picks
her nose

if you miss nose
picking time
then you must collect
three and one half milograms
of toe jam
and give it to barbara's cat

and if you can't find
barbara's cat

then how you gonna call
yourself
a black man?

Black Power
(For All the Beautiful Black Panthers East)

But the whole thing is a miracle—See?

We were just standing there
talking—not touching or smoking
Pot
When this cop told
Tyrone
Move along buddy—take your whores
outa here

And this tremendous growl
From out of nowhere
Pounced on him

Nobody to this very day
Can explain
How it happened

And none of the zoos or circuses
Within fifty miles
Had reported
A panther
Missing

Seduction

one day
you gonna walk in this house
and i'm gonna have on a long African
gown
you'll sit down and say "The Black . . . "
and i'm gonna take one arm out
then you—not noticing me at all—will say "What about
this brother . . . "
and i'm going to be slipping it over my head
and you'll rapp on about "The revolution . . . "
while i rest your hand against my stomach
you'll go on—as you always do—saying
"I just can't dig . . . "
while i'm moving your hand up and down
and i'll be taking your dashiki off
then you'll say "What we really need . . ."
and i'll be licking your arm
and "The way I see it we ought to . . . "
and unbuckling your pants
"And what about the situation . . . "
and taking your shorts off
then you'll notice
your state of undress
and knowing you you'll just say
"Nikki,
isn't this counterrevolutionary. . . ?"

Word Poem
(Perhaps Worth Considering)

as things be/come
let's destroy
then we can destroy
what we be/come
let's build
what we become
when we dream

2

Black Judgement

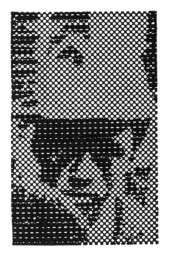

The Dance Committee
(Concerning Jean-Leon Destiné)

I am the token negro
I sit in the colored section with Fanon in hand
(to demonstrate my militancy)
and a very dry martini
(ingredients: yellow grass and a green faggot
over lightly)
while circumcised flies buzz brassy smells over my head

The women (obviously my superiors)
White sharp lines
and light-blue mascara
reaching all the way down beyond the red neck
crossing the middle age spread
form a double V (at home and the office)
spinning spidery daydreams of cloth
once covering and once removed
dripping babies

I asked why
the group wouldn't be in the Black community
(it was Black french—which I should point out
has nothing to do with sex)
And was told quite soundlee

that just because they're colored don't
mean they're not artists too
THEY'RE ARTISTS TOO AND COLOR
AIN'T GOT NOTHING TO DO WITH IT
AND WHY OH WHY WON'T YOU PEOPLE
LET US FORGET YOU'RE COLORED TOO

Token negroes
I do believe, at least I was told,
and it is very important
for future exchanges
And again I must point out sex is not the issue
that we should simply fuck
tokenism

Of Liberation

Dykes of the world are united
Faggots got their thing together
(Everyone is organized)
Black people these are facts
Where's your power

Honkies rule the world
Where's your power Black people
(There are those who say it's found in the root of all evil)
You are money
You seek property
Own yourself
3/5 of a man
100% whore
Chattel property
All of us
The most vital commodity in america
Is Black people
Ask any circumcised honkie

There are relevant points to be considered, Black People
Honkies tell niggers don't burn
"violence begets you nothing my fellow americans"
But they insist on straightened hair
They insist on bleaching creams
It is only natural that we would escalate

It has been pointed out:
"If we can't out fight them, we can't out vote them"
These are relevant points to consider
If 10% honkies can run south africa
            then
10% Black people (which has nothing to do with negroes)
can run america
These are facts
Deal with them

It has been pointed out:
"The last bastion of white supremacy
is in the Black man's mind"
(Note—this is not a criticism of brothers)

Everything comes in steps
Negative step one: get the white out of your hair
Negative step two: get the white out of your mind
Negative step three: get the white out of your parties
Negative step four: get the white out of your meetings

BLACK STEP ONE:
Get the feeling out (this may be painful—endure)
BLACK STEP TWO:
Outline and implement the program
All honkies and some negroes will have to die
This is unfortunate but necessary

Black law must be implemented
The Black Liberation Front must take responsibility
For Black people
If the choice is between the able and the faithful
The faithful must be chosen
Blackness is its own qualifier
Blackness is its own standard

There are no able negroes
White degrees do not qualify negroes to run
The Black Revolution

The Black Liberation Front must set the standards
These are international rules

Acquaint yourself with the Chinese, The Vietnamese,
The Cubans
And other Black Revolutions
We have tried far too long to ally with whites
Remember the rule of thumb:
WILD ANIMALS CAN BE TRAINED
BUT NEVER TAMED
The honkie is this category
Like any beast he can be trained with varying degrees
of excellence to
1) eat from a table
2) wash his hands
3) drive an automobile or bicycle
4) run a machine
5) And in some rare cases has been known to speak
This is training, Black people
And while it is amusing
It is still a circus we are watching
Barnum and Bailey are the minds
behind president Johnson

You would not trust your life to a wolf or tiger
no matter how many tricks they can learn
You would not turn your back on a cobra
Even if it can dance
Do not trust a honkie
They are all of the same family
The Black Liberation Front has free jobs to offer

for those concerned about the unemployed
The sisters need to make flags
(there are no nations without a flag)
The Red Black and Green must wave from all our
buildings as we build our nation
Even the winos have a part—they empty the bottles
    which the children can collect
Teen-age girls can fill with flammable liquid
and stuff with a rag
Professor Neal says a tampax will do just fine
Ammunition for gun and mind must be smuggled in
Support your local bookstore
Dashikis hide a multitude of Revolution
Support your local dress shop

As all reports have indicated our young men are primary
On the job training is necessary
Support your local rebellion—
send a young man into the streets

Our churches must bless these efforts in the name
of our Black God
Far too long we have been like Jesus
Crucified
It is time for The Resurrection of Blackness
"A little child shall lead them" for the Bible tells me so
And we shall follow our children into battle

Our choice a decade ago was war or dishonor
(another word for integration)
We chose dishonor
We got war

Mistakes are a fact of life
It is the response to error that counts

Erase our errors with the Black Flame
Purify our neighborhoods with the Black Flame
We are the artists of this decade
Draw a new picture with the Black Flame
Live a new life within the Black Flame

Our choice now is war or death
Our option is survival
Listen to your own Black hearts

Poem for Black Boys
(With Special Love to James)

Where are your heroes, my little Black ones
You are the Indian you so disdainfully shoot
Not the big bad sheriff on his faggoty white horse

You should play run-away-slave
or Mau Mau
These are more in line with your history

Ask your mothers for a Rap Brown gun
Santa just may comply if you wish hard enough
Ask for CULLURD instead of Monopoly
DO NOT SIT IN DO NOT FOLLOW KING
GO DIRECTLY TO STREETS
This is a game you can win

As you sit there with your all understanding eyes
You know the truth of what I'm saying
Play Back-to-Black
Grow a natural and practice vandalism
These are useful games (some say a skill is even learned)

There is a new game I must tell you of
It's called Catch The Leader Lying
(and knowing your sense of the absurd
you will enjoy this)

Also a company called Revolution has just issued
a special kit for little boys
called Burn Baby
I'm told it has full instructions on how to siphon gas
and fill a bottle

Then our old friend Hide and Seek becomes valid
Because we have much to seek and ourselves to hide
from a lecherous dog

And this poem I give is worth much more
than any nickel bag
or ten cent toy
And you will understand all too soon
That you, my children of battle, are your heroes
You must invent your own games and teach us old ones
how to play

Concerning
One Responsible Negro
with Too Much Power

scared?
are responsible negroes running
scared?

i understand i'm to be sued
and you say you can't fight fifteen hundred national
guards men
so you'll beat the shit
out of poor Black me
(no doubt because i've castrated you)

dynamite came to your attention
and responsible negroes tell the cops

your tongue must be removed
since you have no brain
to keep it in check

aren't you turned around
teaching tolerance

how can i tolerate
genocide
my cup is full
and you already know
we have no ability
to delay gratification

i only want to reclaim myself
i even want you
to reclaim yourself
but more and more i'm being convinced
that your death
responsible negro
is the first step
toward my reclamation

it's very sad
i'd normally stop and cry
but evening is coming
and i've got to negotiate
for my people's freedom

Reflections on April 4, 1968

What can I, a poor Black woman, do to destroy america? This is a question, with appropriate variations, being asked in every Black heart. There is one answer—I can kill. There is one compromise—I can protect those who kill. There is one cop-out—I can encourage others to kill. There are no other ways.

The assassination of Martin Luther King is an act of war. President johnson, your friendly uncandidate, has declared war on Black people. He is not making any distinction between us and negroes. The question—does it have rhythm? The answer—yes. The response—kill it. They have been known to shoot at the wind and violate the earth's gravity for these very reasons.

Obviously the first step toward peace is the removal of at least two fingers, and most probably three, from both hands of all white people. Fingers that are not controlled must be removed. This is the first step toward a true and lasting peace. We would also suggest blinding or the removal of at least two eyes from one of the heads of all albino freaks.

And some honkie asked about the reaction? What do you people want? Isn't it enough that you killed him? You want to tell me how to mourn? You want to determine and qualify how I, a lover, should respond to the death of my beloved?

May he rest in peace. May his blood choke the life from ten hundred million whites. May the warriors in the streets go ever forth into the stores for guns and tv's, for whatever makes them happy (for only a happy people make successful Revolution) and this day begin the Black Revolution.

How can one hundred and fifty policemen allow a man to be shot? Police were seen coming from the direction of the shots. And there was no conspiracy? Just as there was no violent reaction to his death. And no city official regretted his death but only that it occurred in Memphis. We heard similar statements from Dallas—this country has too many large Southern cities.

Do not be fooled, Black people. Johnson's footprints are the footprints of death. He came in on a death, he is presiding over a death and his own death should take him out. Let us pray for the whole state of Christ's church.

Zeus has wrestled the Black Madonna and he is down for the count. Intonations to nadinolia gods and a slain honkie will not overcome. Let america's baptism be the fire this time. Any comic book can tell you if you fill a room with combustible materials then close it up tight it will catch fire. This is a thirsty fire they have created. It will not be squelched until it destroys them. Such is the nature of revolution.

America has called itself the promised land—and themselves God's chosen people. This is where we come in, Black people. God's chosen people have always had to suffer—to endure—to overcome. We have suffered and america has been rewarded. This is a foul equation. We must now seek our reward. God will not love us unless we share with others our suffering. Precious Lord—Take Our Hands—Lead Us On.

The Funeral of
Martin Luther King, Jr.

His headstone said
FREE AT LAST, FREE AT LAST
But death is a slave's freedom
We seek the freedom of free men
And the construction of a world
Where Martin Luther King could have lived
and preached non-violence

A Litany for Peppe

They had a rebellion in Washington this year
because white people killed Martin Luther King
Even the cherry blossoms wouldn't appear

Black Power and a sweet Black Peace

Just about 200 white people died
because they conspired to kill Martin Luther King

And peace and power to you my child

Blessed be machine guns in Black hands
All power to grenades that destroy our oppressor
Peace Peace, Black Peace at all costs

We're having our spring sale
200 honkies for one non-violent

Even Wilmington Delaware
(a funni negro at best)
Responded appropriately

And to you my Black boy
A Revolution
My gift of love
Blessed is he who kills
For he shall control this earth

Nikki-Rosa

childhood remembrances are always a drag
if you're Black
you always remember things like living in Woodlawn
with no inside toilet
and if you become famous or something
they never talk about how happy you were to have
your mother
all to yourself and
how good the water felt when you got your bath
from one of those
big tubs that folk in chicago barbecue in
and somehow when you talk about home
it never gets across how much you
understood their feelings
as the whole family attended meetings about Hollydale
and even though you remember
your biographers never understand
your father's pain as he sells his stock
and another dream goes
And though you're poor it isn't poverty that
concerns you
and though they fought a lot
it isn't your father's drinking that makes any difference
but only that everybody is together and you

and your sister have happy birthdays and very good
Christmasses
and I really hope no white person ever has cause
to write about me
because they never understand
Black love is Black wealth and they'll
probably talk about my hard childhood
and never understand that
all the while I was quite happy

The Great Pax Whitie

In the beginning was the word
And the word was
Death
And the word was nigger
And the word was death to all niggers
And the word was death to all life
And the word was death to all
   peace be still

The genesis was life
The genesis was death
In the genesis of death
Was the genesis of war
   be still peace be still

In the name of peace
They waged the wars
   ain't they got no shame

In the name of peace
Lot's wife is now a product of the Morton company
   nah, they ain't got no shame

Noah packing his wife and kiddies up for a holiday
row row row your boat

But why'd you leave the unicorns, noah
Huh? why'd you leave them
While our Black Madonna stood there
Eighteen feet high holding Him in her arms
Listening to the rumblings of peace
   be still be still

CAN I GET A WITNESS? WITNESS? WITNESS?
He wanted to know
And peter only asked who is that dude?
Who is that Black dude?
Looks like a troublemaker to me
And the foundations of the mighty mighty
Ro Man Cat holic church were laid

   hallelujah jesus
   nah, they ain't got no shame

Cause they killed the Carthaginians
in the great appian way
And they killed the Moors
"to civilize a nation"
And they just killed the earth
And blew out the sun
In the name of a god
Whose genesis was white
And war wooed god
And america was born
Where war became peace
And genocide patriotism
And honor is a happy slave
cause all god's chillun need rhythm
And glory hallelujah why can't peace
   be still

The great emancipator was a bigot
  ain't they got no shame
And making the world safe for democracy
Were twenty million slaves
  nah, they ain't got no shame

And they barbecued six million
To raise the price of beef
And crossed the 16th parallel
To control the price of rice
  ain't we never gonna see the light

And champagne was shipped out of the East
While kosher pork was introduced
To Africa
  Only the torch can show the way

In the beginning was the deed
And the deed was death

And the honkies are getting confused
  peace be still

So the great white prince
Was shot like a nigger in texas
And our Black shining prince was murdered
like that thug in his cathedral
While our nigger in memphis
was shot like their prince in dallas
And my lord
ain't we never gonna see the light
The rumblings of this peace must be stilled
  be stilled be still

ahh Black people
ain't we got no pride?

Intellectualism

sometimes i feel like i just get in
everybody's way
when i was a little girl
i use to go read
or make fudge
when i got bigger i
read
or picked my nose
that's what they called
intelligence
or when i got older
intellectualism
but it was only
that i was in the way

Universality

You see boy
is universal
It can be a
man
a woman
a child
or anything—
but normally it's
a
nigger
I was told

Knoxville, Tennessee

I always like summer
best
you can eat fresh corn
from daddy's garden
and okra
and greens
and cabbage
and lots of
barbecue
and buttermilk
and homemade ice-cream
at the church picnic
and listen to
gospel music
outside
at the church
homecoming
and go to the mountains with
your grandmother
and go barefooted
and be warm
all the time
not only when you go to bed
and sleep

Records

it's so important to record
i sit here trying to record
trying to find a new profound
way to say
johnson is the vilest
germiest beast
the world has ever
known
in the alleged civilized
times
trying to record
how i feel about a
family
being wiped out
trying to explain
that they have nothing
against bobby
he's a white
millionaire
several hundred times over
so it must be me
they are killing
trying to record
the feeling of shame
that we Black people

haven't yet
committed a
major assassination
which very desperately
must be
done
trying to record the
ignorance of the
voices
that say
i'm glad a negro
didn't do it
a negro needs to kill
something
trying to record
that this country must be
destroyed
if we are to live
must be destroyed if we are to live
must be destroyed if we are to live

Adulthood
(For Claudia)

i usta wonder who i'd be
when i was a little girl in indianapolis
sitting on doctors porches with post-dawn pre-debs
(wondering would my aunt drag me to church sunday)
i was meaningless
and i wondered if life
would give me a chance to mean

i found a new life in the withdrawal from all things
not like my image

when i was a teen-ager i usta sit
on front steps conversing
the gym teacher's son with embryonic eyes
about the essential essence of the universe
(and other bullshit stuff)
recognizing the basic powerlessness of me

but then i went to college where i learned
that just because everything i was was unreal
i could be real and not just real through withdrawal
into emotional crosshairs or colored bourgeois
intellectual pretensions

but from involvement with things approaching reality
i could possibly have a life

so catatonic emotions and time wasting sex games
were replaced with functioning commitments to logic
and
necessity and the gray area was slowly darkened into
a Black thing

for a while progress was being made along with a certain
degree
of happiness cause i wrote a book and found a love
and organized a theatre and even gave some lectures on
Black history
and began to believe all good people could get
together and win without bloodshed
then
hammarskjöld was killed
and lumumba was killed
and diem was killed
and kennedy was killed
and malcolm was killed
and evers was killed
and schwerner, chaney and goodman were killed
and liuzzo was killed
and stokely fled the country
and le roi was arrested
and rap was arrested
and pollard, thompson and cooper were killed
and king was killed
and kennedy was killed
and i sometimes wonder why i didn't become a
debutante
sitting on porches, going to church all the time,
wondering

is my eye make-up on straight
or a withdrawn discoursing on the stars and moon
instead of a for real Black person who must now feel
and inflict
pain

From a Logical Point of View

I mean it's only natural that if
water seeks its own level
The honkie would not bother with
Viet Nam
It's unworthy of him
Cause they are not ready
for the revolutionary
advanced technology
that america is trying
to put on them
and nothing is worse
than a
dream deferred

It's just those simple
agrarian people
trying to invoke
simple land
reform
and maybe bring
a new level
of consciousness
to their people

And here america is
trying
to teach them
how to
read and
write
and be
capitalists
when it's fairly obvious
to the naked
untrained
eye
that they aren't
ready
for meaningful
change
and the revolution
is only
in the honkies'
mind

I mean
if it was me
I wouldn't
try to enlighten
those
slant-eyed
bastards
who only want
to sing and
dance
and be happy
all the time
I would have had enough fooling
around with niggers

I mean really
if I had at my
disposal
a means to get
out of this world
I'd go
and let those un
grateful
coloreds
try to get
along
without
me

Dreams

in my younger years
before i learned
black people aren't
suppose to dream
i wanted to be
a raelet
and say "dr o wn d in my youn tears"
or "tal kin bout tal kin bout"
or marjorie hendricks and grind
all up against the mic
and scream
"baaaaaby nightandday
baaaaaby nightandday"
then as i grew and matured
i became more sensible
and decided i would
settle down
and just become
a sweet inspiration

Revolutionary Music

you've just got to dig sly
and the family stone
damn the words
you gonna be dancing to the music
james brown can go to
viet nam
or sing about whatever he
has to
since he already told
the honkie
"although you happy you better try
to get along
money won't change you
but time is taking you on"
not to mention
doing a whole
song they can't even snap
their fingers to
"good god! ugh!"
talking bout
"i got the feeling baby i got the feeling"
and "hey everybody let me tell you the news"
martha and the vandellas dancing in the streets
while shorty long is functioning at that junction
yeah we hip to that

aretha said they better
think
but she already said
"ain't no way to love you"
(and you know she wasn't talking to us)
and dig the o'jays asking "must i always be a stand in
for love"
i mean they say "i'm a fool for being myself"

While the mighty mighty impressions have told the
world
for once and for all
"We're a Winner"
even our names—le roi has said—are together
impressions
temptations
supremes
delfonics
miracles
intruders (i mean intruders?)
not beatles and animals and white bad things like
young rascals and shit
we be digging all
our revolutionary music consciously or un
cause sam cooke said "a change is gonna come"

Beautiful Black Men
(With compliments and apologies to all not mentioned by name)

i wanta say just gotta say something
bout those beautiful beautiful beautiful outasight
black men
with they afros
walking down the street
is the same ol danger
but a brand new pleasure

sitting on stoops, in bars, going to offices
running numbers, watching for their whores
preaching in churches, driving their hogs
walking their dogs, winking at me
in their fire red, lime green, burnt orange
royal blue tight tight pants that hug
what i like to hug

jerry butler, wilson pickett, the impressions
temptations, mighty mighty sly
don't have to do anything but walk
on stage
and i scream and stamp and shout
see new breed men in breed alls
dashiki suits with shirts that match
the lining that complements the ties
that smile at the sandals
where dirty toes peek at me
and i scream and stamp and shout
for more beautiful beautiful beautiful
black men with outasight afros

Woman Poem

you see, my whole life
is tied up
to unhappiness
it's father cooking breakfast
and me getting fat as a hog
or having no food
at all and father proving
his incompetence
again
i wish i knew how it would feel
to be free

it's having a job
they won't let you work
or no work at all
castrating me
(yes it happens to women too)

it's a sex object if you're pretty
and no love
or love and no sex if you're fat
get back fat black woman be a mother
grandmother strong thing but not woman
gameswoman romantic woman love needer
man seeker dick eater sweat getter
fuck needing love seeking woman

it's a hole in your shoe
and buying lil' sis a dress
and her saying you shouldn't
when you know
all too well—that you shouldn't

but smiles are only something we give
to properly dressed social workers
not each other
only smiles of i know
your game sister
which isn't really
a smile

joy is finding a pregnant roach
and squashing it
not finding someone to hold
let go get off get back don't turn
me on you black dog
how dare you care
about me
you ain't got no good sense
cause i ain't shit you must be lower
than that to care

it's a filthy house
with yesterday's watermelon
and monday's tears
cause true ladies don't
know how to clean

it's intellectual devastation
of everybody
to avoid emotional commitment

"yeah honey i would've married
him but he didn't have no degree"

its knock-kneed mini-skirted
wig wearing died blond mamma's scar
born dead my scorn your whore
rough heeled broken nailed powdered
face me
whose whole life is tied
up to unhappiness
cause it's the only
for real thing
i
know

Ugly Honkies, or
The Election Game
and How to Win It

ever notice how it's only the ugly
honkies
who hate
like hitler was an ugly dude
same with lyndon
ike nixon hhh wallace maddox
and all the governors of mississippi
and you don't ever see a good-looking
cop
perhaps this only relates to the physical
nature of the beast
at best interesting for a beast
and never beautiful
by that black standard

if dracula came to town now
he'd look like daley
booing senator ribicoff
no pretty man himself
but at least out of the beast
category

yet all had to describe julian bond
as the handsome black legislator
which is, of course, redundant

life put muskie and huskie humphrey
on the cover
and we were struck by a thought:
"if we must be screwed—they could at least be pretty"
but the uglies kill
all the pretties
like john and bobby
and evers and king
and if caroline don't look
out she'll be next

arthur miller spoke of the white things
jumping wildly on their feet
banging their paws together
hating the young
only this time they were hating
their young
a salute to the chicago kids
now you and the world knows
we weren't lying
a cracked skull in time
may save mine
(though i doubt it)
and hhh says we ought to quit pretending
what daley did was wrong
We aren't pretending
We didn't give a damn
you guys ought to get yourselves
together
eating your kids is a sexual
perversion

the politics of '68 remind us grievously
of the politics of '64
the deal to put the bird
and his faggoty flock in the white nest
(which began in dallas)
is being replayed and repaid
(the downpayment being made in los angeles)
with tricky dicky to win this time
(the final payment chicago)
cause there's only two parties in this country
anti-nigger and pro-nigger
most of the pro-niggers are now dead
this second reconstruction is being aborted
as was the first
the pro-niggers council voting
the anti-niggers have guns
if we vote this season we ought to seek to make it
effective
the barrel of a gun is the best
voting machine
your best protest vote
is a dead honkie
much more effective than a yes
for gregory or cleaver

this negative bullshit
they run on us
is to tie us up in identification
"you don't want nixon-agnew do you?"
"well vote for humphrey-muskie"
but all you honkies are alien
to me
and i reject the choice
it's the same game they run
about nigeria

"whose side are you on?"
the black side, fool
how many times must i show that?
taking sides is identifying
and that is commitment
be committed to us
and don't deal with them
as long as we chose one evil over another
(on some bullshit theory that it's lesser)
we'll have bullshit evil to deal with
let's build a for real black thing
called revolution
known to revolutionists as
love

the obvious need is a new liberal white party
to organize liberal and radical honkies
this will lessen but not remove the clear and present
danger
to us
we need to continue our fight to control
all of america
honkies are just not fit to rule
these are sorry but true facts—not one honkie is fit to
rule
the worse junkie or black businessman is more humane
than the best honkie
no black person would have allowed
his troops to be so slaughtered
and before you scream "king king"
his promise was your picture in the paper
and your head in bandages
mccarthy (the administration's official dissident
candidate)
was not so honest

there are those who say he begun with lyndon's blessings
and the promise of good speaking engagements
and since we have witnessed the assassination of one who
didn't need the money
or have the blessing
we are inclined to agree

and daley talked of teddy not making up his mind
he said no
that's pretty definite

only it's sad that once again
we have a chance we aren't fully
utilizing
the honkies are at war to decide what to do
about us
and here we are
trying to get
into what every sensible person should be running
from
when we integrated the schools
they began moving away from public education
when we integrated the churches
they started the god is dead bit
now we're integrating politics
and they're moving to a police state
we ought to beat them to the punch
and pull off our coup
and take over, with arms and everything necessary,
our communities

post-election note:

those of us breathing easy now that wallace
wasn't elected

check again
that's gas you're smelling
survival is still the name of the game
black people still our only allies
life or death still our only option
let's me and you do that thing
please?

Cultural Awareness

as we all probably realize
on some level
people are basically selfish
and perhaps in some cases
a little more than thoughtless
mostly i would suppose
because of the nature of life
under this and most other
systems

but someone came by
and brought to my attention
how ridiculously mean
i was being

most people
he assured me
have followed the teachings
of the honorable maulana elijah el shabazz
and do not have anything at all
to do with pork

and here he found
when visiting me
that i didn't have
zig-zag papers
for a kosher
substitute

For Saundra

i wanted to write
a poem
that rhymes
but revolution doesn't lend
itself to be-bopping

then my neighbor
who thinks i hate
asked—do you ever write
tree poems—i like trees
so i thought
i'll write a beautiful green tree poem
peeked from my window
to check the image
noticed the school yard was covered
with asphalt
no green—no trees grow
in manhattan

then, well, i thought the sky
i'll do a big blue sky poem
but all the clouds have winged
low since no-Dick was elected

so i thought again
and it occurred to me

maybe i shouldn't write
at all
but clean my gun
and check my kerosene supply

perhaps these are not poetic
times
at all

Balances

in life
one is always
balancing

like we juggle our mothers
against our fathers

or one teacher
against another
(only to balance our grade average)

3 grains salt
to one ounce truth

our sweet black essence
or the funky honkies down the street

and lately i've begun wondering
if you're trying to tell me something

we used to talk all night
and do things alone together

and i've begun
(as a reaction to a feeling)
to balance
the pleasure of loneliness
against the pain
of loving you

For a Poet I Know

if you sang songs i could make a request
does the same hold true of poems

i'd like a poem about me
i'm black and exist and for real
i'd like a poem about your uncle
who got out of his bed to let us screw
yeah and maybe a poem
about how i tried
to talk to you one night
and you suggested i read my own poems
what were you really thinking

i'd like to hear a poem about your wig
everybody's got a wig
aretha's is on her head
james brown's is humphrey
mine is columbia
yours is the college you teach at
or the people who sent you there

i want a poem telling how tired you are
of fucking women
and relating to your hospital
experiences

or maybe a poem about who you'd like
to lay beside and dream with
and a real long poem on what you dream about

i really need a rare book poem
and what they mean to you
and a new book poem about what you read
and a joe goncalves poem about a hardworking brother
and a carolyn rodgers poem about a beautiful sister
and a father poem for hoyt fuller
and a jet poem because we've never been in it
and a scared poem about me taking your clothes off
then offering an excuse
and a man poem about how you reached your Blackness
or perhaps an alcoholic poem about your mother
and a climbing poem about how you reached the heights
and a you poem mostly
cause your other poems
don't tell me who you are
and i
having felt and tasted you know
what you should know and relate to
that you should write and are capable of writing
a tall lean explosive poem
not just a quiet half white hating poem
about a black poem
called a black poet
that i know and would like to love
again

For Theresa

and when i was all alone
facing my adolescence
looking forward
to cleaning house
and reading books
and maybe learning bridge
so that i could fit
into acceptable society
acceptably
you came along
and loved me
for being black and bitchy
hateful and scared
and you came along
and cared that i got
all the things necessary
to adulthood
and even made sure
i wouldn't hate
my mother
or father
and you even understood
that i should love
peppe
but not too much

and give to gary
but not all of me
and keep on moving
'til i found me
and now you're sick
and have been hurt
for some time
and i've felt guilty
and impotent
for not being able
to give yourself
to you
as you gave
yourself
to me

My Poem

i am 25 years old
black female poet
wrote a poem asking
nigger can you kill
if they kill me
it won't stop
the revolution

i have been robbed
it looked like they knew
that i was to be hit
they took my tv
my two rings
my piece of african print
and my two guns
if they take my life
it won't stop
the revolution

my phone is tapped
my mail is opened
they've caused me to turn
on all my old friends
and all my new lovers

if i hate all black
people
and all negroes
it won't stop
the revolution

i'm afraid to tell
my roommate where i'm going
and scared to tell
people if i'm coming
if i sit here
for the rest
of my life
it won't stop
the revolution

if i never write
another poem
or short story
if i flunk out
of grad school
if my car is reclaimed
and my record player
won't play
and if i never see
a peaceful day
or do a meaningful
black thing
it won't stop
the revolution

the revolution
is in the streets
and if i stay on
the 5th floor

it will go on
if i never do
anything
it will go on

Black Judgements
(Of bullshit niggerish ways)

You
with your bullshit niggerish ways
want to destroy me

You want to preach
responsible revolution
along with progressive
procreation

Your desires will not be honored
this season

Shivering under the armour
of your
white protector
fear not
for thou art evil
The audacity of wanting
to be near the life
of what you seek to kill

Can you love
can you hate
is your game any damn good

Black Judgements are upon you
Black Judgements are upon you